EARLY PRINTED BOOKS

EARLY PRINTED BOOKS

IN THE LIBRARY OF

ST CATHARINE'S COLLEGE
CAMBRIDGE

J. B. BILDERBECK, M.A.

LIBRARIAN

CAMBRIDGE:
AT THE UNIVERSITY PRESS
1911

CAMBRIDGE
UNIVERSITY PRESS

University Printing House, Cambridge CB2 8BS, United Kingdom

Published in the United States of America by Cambridge University Press, New York

Cambridge University Press is part of the University of Cambridge.

It furthers the University's mission by disseminating knowledge in the pursuit of education, learning and research at the highest international levels of excellence.

www.cambridge.org
Information on this title: www.cambridge.org/9781107421462

© Cambridge University Press 1911

First published 1911
First paperback edition 2014

A catalogue record for this publication is available from the British Library

ISBN 978-1-107-42146-2 Paperback

PREFACE

THIS list, for the most part, relates to books which were printed before 1521, but includes *three* of later date from the presses of Pynson and Wynkyn de Worde. In respect to the grouping and order of the presses, Proctor's lists have, generally, been followed, presses not in his lists being entered under their respective localities after the others; but, on the other hand, no distinction has been made between London and Westminster, Nos. 46, 47, 48 have been entered under Kerver and not under Georg Wolf, and No. 63 should perhaps have been entered later, as this book appears to have been printed by Nic. de Benedictis alone. (*See* Proctor: Lyon—press XXIX.)

Descriptions of some of the older bindings have been given, together with plates representing the binding of No. 4—Koberger's Bible—and also some of the stamps on Nos. 3, 14, 16, 63.

An attempt has been made to throw light on the history of individual books, and at the end of the Catalogue is an *Index* of inscribed names and donors, followed by short notes on some of the persons named. As bearing on this matter, it may be well to state that among the College records are several old catalogues of different dates relating to the books in the Library. The earliest of these, a list of the MSS. presented to the College by its founder, formed the subject of the first paper ever published by the Cambridge Antiquarian Society (1840). There are catalogues of 1633 and 1698 and, subsequent to these, a much more extensive catalogue which was written out probably about 1715 during the Mastership of Thos. Sherlock. In the book containing the latter have also been entered (i) a list of the books given to the Library in 1718 by John Addenbrooke, Fellow of the College and Founder of the Hospital in Cambridge, and (ii) a list of the books presented in 1728 by Thos. Crosse, who was Master from 1719 to 1736. The 1715 catalogue apparently continued in use till superseded by the printed catalogue of 1771 —which, perhaps, may claim the distinction of being the earliest printed *general* catalogue of a library in the University of Cambridge. This printed catalogue includes the books that had come to the College in 1761 by the bequest of Thos. Sherlock, Bishop of London, a separate list of which is also among the records.

I acknowledge with gratitude my obligations to many for the assistance they have rendered me. In particular am I much indebted to Mr F. J. H. Jenkinson for his friendly guidance and readiness to help, to Mr C. E. Sayle for valuable advice and many acts of courtesy, and to Mr Alfred Rogers for his kindly assistance in the decipherment of some of the inscriptions. Mr A. W. Spratt and Mr W. H. S. Jones of S. Catharine's College have helped me in connexion with some of the Greek books, and I tender my thanks to them and also to the Provost of King's College, Dr W. W. Greg of Trinity College, Rev. G. A. S. Schneider of Gonville and Caius College and Mr S. Gaselee of Magdalene College for their courtesy in providing me with facilities for the examination of books in the libraries of their several colleges. In the biographical notes at the end of the *Indexes* I have embodied information courteously supplied, the source of which has in every case been indicated, but I must express my gratitude more particularly to Dr J. Venn, F.R.S., for his readiness to help and the opportunities he gave me of consulting him, to his son Mr J. A. Venn for kindly permitting me to make use of information contained in the University Matriculation lists for 1544–1658 which he has now in preparation, and to Rev. W. Greenwood for allowing me on different occasions to examine the early Registers of S. Benet's, Cambridge.

J. B. BILDERBECK.

March, 1911.

ABBREVIATIONS

(A) Books referred to: (B) Words and Phrases

(A)

Alum. Oxon.	Joseph Foster: Alumni Oxonienses 1500–1714.
Blades.	W. Blades: The biography and typography of Wm Caxton. 2nd edn. 8°. Lond. 1882.
Brunet.	J. C. Brunet: Manuel du libraire et de l'amateur de livres. 6 tom. Paris, 1860–65. With Supplément (P. Deschamps). 2 tom. Paris, 1878–80.
Campbell.	M. F. A. G. Campbell: Annales de la typographie néerlandaise au XVᵉ siècle. 1874.
Coll. rec.	S. Catharine's College records.
Coop.	C. H. and Thompson Cooper: Athenæ Cantabrigienses. 2 vols. Camb. 1856, 1861.
C. or *Cop.*	W. A. Copinger: Supplement to Hain's Repertorium bibliographicum. 2 pts in 3 vols. Lond. 1895–
D.N.B.	Dictionary of National Biography.
Duff.	E. Gordon Duff: Printers, stationers and bookbinders of Westminster and London 1476–1535.
Grad. Cant.	Graduati Cantabrigienses sive catalogus 1659–1823.
Gray.	G. J. Gray: The earlier Cambridge stationers and bookbinders and the first Cambridge printer. Oxford, 1904.
H.	L. Hain: Repertorium bibliographicum. 4 vols. 1826–1838.
Heitz.	Heitz and Bernoulli: Basler Büchermarken bis zum Anfang des 17. Jahrhunderts. Strassburg, 1895.
Holtrop.	J. W. Holtrop: Monuments typographiques des Pays Bas au quinzième siècle. 1868.
King's.	List of the incunabula in the library of King's College, Cambridge. 1908.
Krist.	Paul Kristeller: Die italienischen Buchdrucker- und Verlegerzeichen bis 1525. Strassburg, 1893.
Le Neve.	John Le Neve: Fasti Ecclesiae Anglicanae...corrected by T. Duffus Hardy. 3 vols. Oxford, 1854.
Monast. Anglic.	W. Dugdale: Monasticon Anglicanum. 8 vols. (vol. VI. in 3 parts). Lond. 1846.
Morg.	Catalogue of manuscripts and early printed books...in the library of Pierpont Morgan. 3 vols. Lond. 1907.

Neale.	C. M. Neale: The early Honors Lists of the University of Cambridge. 1909.
Panz.	G. W. Panzer: Annales typographici. 11 tom. 1793–1803.
Pell.	Marie Pellechet: Catalogue général des incunables des bibliothèques publiques de France. 2 tom. A–Commandements. 1897–
Proct.	(i) R. Proctor: Index to the early printed books in the British Museum from the invention of printing to the year M.D. 2 vols. 1898.
	(ii) ...Part II. M.DI–M.DXX, Sect. i. 1903.
Ren. or *Renouard.*	Philippe Renouard: Bibliographie des impressions et des œuvres de Josse Badius Ascensius. 3 vols. 1908.
Sayle.	C. E. Sayle: Early English printed books in the University Library, Cambridge. 4 vols. 1900–
Silv.	L. C. Silvestre: Marques typographiques. 1853–67.
Sinker.	R. Sinker: A catalogue of the fifteenth-century printed books in the library of Trinity College, Cambridge. 1876.
Venn.	J. A. Venn: Cambridge University Matriculation lists 1544–1658 (*in preparation*).
Weale.	W. H. J. Weale: Bookbindings and rubbings of bindings in the National Art Library, South Kensington Museum. 1898.

(B)

Goth.	Gothic letter.	ref.	reference.
Rom.	Roman letter.	sur.	surrounding.
col.	columns.	c. sig.	with signatures.
f., ff.	leaf, leaves.	s. sig.	without signatures.
li.	lines.	c. ff. n.	leaves numbered.
comment.	commentary.	s. ff. n.	leaves not numbered.
marg.	marginal matter.	n. d.	without date.

Plates I. A, I. B.......Binding of No. 4.
Plate II. ....Stamps on bindings of Nos. 3, 14, 16, 63.

GERMANY.

STRASSBURG.

Johann Prüss.

1. 1486. Biblia Latina.

(N.B.—Place and printer not indicated.)

F°. 271 mm. (over-cropped to injury of headlines). C. sig. S. ff. n. Text: 2 col. 48 li. Interpretations of Hebrew names: 3 col. 52, 53 li. Marg. in New Test. only. Coloured initials.

Colln. Bible: a–z⁸ (a I wanting), aa–cc⁸, dd⁶, ee–zz⁸, A–E⁸, FG¹⁰, H–T⁸, UX⁶=(534–1)=533 ff. Canons and interpretations: Y⁸, AA–DD⁸, EE 1, 2, 3, 4 (remaining leaves wanting) = 44 ff. H 8ᵃ at top "Registrum" for "Mattheus"; I 7ᵃ matter at end of first col. apparently cancelled and paper pasted over; O 2 signed P 2; Q 3 "Corinthos II." for "Galathas"; Q 5ᵃ "Philippenes" for "Ephesios"; Colophon after Apocalypse; Y I not signed.

Bound between (i) *Book of Common Prayer*, 1662 (John Bill and Christ. Barker), and (ii) *The whole book of Psalms collected into English meeter*, 1661 (Sternhold, Hopkins and others).

Bequest of Bp Sherlock.

H, C. *3093. Pell. 2320. Proct. 517.

Printer of the 1483 Jordanus de Quedlingburg.

2. 25 Aug. 1495. Vocabularius breuiloquus cum arte diphthongandi punctandi et accentuandi.

F°. 277 mm. C. sig. S. ff. n. 2 col. 52 li.

Colln. Aa⁶, abcd⁸, e⁶, fg⁸, h⁶, ik⁸, l⁶, mn⁸, o⁶, p⁸, q⁶, r⁸, s⁶, t⁸, v⁶, x⁸, y⁶, z⁸, A⁶, B⁸, CDE⁶, F⁸, GH⁶, I⁸, KL⁶, M⁸, N⁶, O⁸, P⁶, Q⁸, RS⁶, T⁸, V⁶, X⁸, Y⁵ (Y 6 wanting), = 321 ff.

Rebound, in original boards, stamped leather much rubbed, and remains of clasps.

On Aa Iᵃ "Pertinet ad R. Stevenson"; below "Et jam pertinet Ricō Wilberham ex dono predicti Reginalldi Stevenson." In 1698 Cat.

Panz. I. 55, 290. Cop. III. 6298. Proct. 637.

B.

I

KÖLN.

JOHANN KOELHOFF.

3. (1481?) HENRICUS BRUNO, alias de Piro s. Pyro de Colonna : super institutiones.

(N.B.—Year, printer, locality not indicated ; press identified by Mr F. J. H. Jenkinson.)

F°. 275 mm. S. sig. S. ff. n. Catchwords. *Type*, Goth. 20 li. = 93 mm. ; larger type for titles, etc. Width of print 130 mm., except on ff. 224 and 227—108 mm., and on ff. 225, 226—114 mm. Coloured initials.

Colln. 1–5^8 (1 1 wanting), 6, 7^6, 8–14^8, 15^6, 16–19^8, 20^{10}, 21–28^8, 29^{10} = (230 – 1) = 229 ff.

Rebacked, original boards, leather cover and remains of clasps. Frame border formed by 2 sets of 4 intersecting fillets. Between sets of fillets square stamps of a wyvern (Plate II. no. 1). Panel divided by sets of four diagonal fillets ; in full lozenges a circular stamp with flowers of 5 petals, in half lozenges triangular groups of three small circles. The last feature distinctive of Oxford bindings (*Duff*, p. 104).

On f. 1, E. C. Tangley (?). In 1633 Cat.

Cop. Pt II. : 1356. Pell. 3037. Not in Proctor.

NÜRNBERG.

ANTON KOBERGER.

4. 14 Apr. 1478. Biblia Latina.

F°. 410 mm. S. sig. C. ff. n. (exc. first leaf and last quire). 2 col. 51 li., but in Gospels colls. 53 li. and much narrower, with wide margins, and marg. ref. to concordances of Gospels. (N.B. The peculiarity in the setting up of the Gospels first appears in Koberger's 1477 edn. See also No. 64.) Coloured initials in blue or red ; beginning of books larger initials in red, blue and green. On recto of first numbered leaf, illuminated initial with gold leaf ground and details carried down between cols. to foot.

Colln. 1^{12}, 2–22^{10}, 23, 24^6, 25–36^{10}, 37, 38^6, 39–41^{10}, 42, 43^8, 44–48^{10}, 49^6 = 468 ff. Sheets without watermark frequently occur. No. 49 may have been originally a quire of 8 ff., the first and last blank.

Rebacked, with original boards, stamped leather, clasps, and finely worked metal bosses, etc. The *front* and *end boards* are differently stamped. See Plates I. A, B, in which, however, some of the details of the stamping are not very clear, as they have suffered from pressure and rubbing. Round the front board are diamond-shaped compartments, enclosing two-headed eagles, crowned and with wings displayed ; the lozenges of the framed panel enclose (1) a stag at bay, (2) a unicorn ; and at the corners of the diamonds are small incised circles.

On 2nd f. "Clemens Heigham de Giffords est verus possessor huius Libri," and under this "I haue lente this booke vnto my cossen Robt. Rookwood of Couldham Hall in Suff. Esquire," after which "and he is to deliv^r it backe ayaine vnto me when so eu^r I shall call for it. the 12 of Januarij A° 1600." In 1698 Cat., and probably the "Biblia" entered in 1633 Cat.

H, C. 3068. W. A. Copinger, *Incunabula Biblica*, no. 36. Panz. II. 180, 51 Pell. 2296. Proct. 1984.

5. 12 July 1493. HARTMANN SCHEDEL: liber chronicarum.

F°. 470 mm. S. sig. C. ff. n., but quires 1, 2, 3, 55, s. ff. n. Initials coloured in red or blue, and chronicle begins with large initial in red and blue.

Colln. Table: 1, 2^6, 3^8 (first f. of 1 wanting); Chronicle: 4^6, 5–7^4, 8–11^6, 12^2, 13^4, 14–16^6, 17^2, 18, 19^6, 20–25^4, 26–29^6, 30^2, 31^6, 32^4, 33–35^6, 36^2, 37^4, 38–61^6 (61 5, 61 6 blank ff. wanting)=(20−1)+(308−2)=325 ff.

N.B. Quires 42 and 43 are conjecturally described as of 6 ff.; they have not been satisfactorily determined.

On f. 266^b Colophon: "Completo in...Nurembergensi vrbe operi ‖ de hystoriis etatum mundi. ac descriptione vrbium fe‖lix imponitur finis. Collectum...auxilio hartmāni Schedel...Anno x̄ri ‖ Millesimo quadringentesimo nonagesimo tercio. die quarto ‖ mensis Iunii." On 61 4^b is printer's colophon with acknowledgment of the services of the artists and map-drawers Michael Wolgemut and Wilhelm Pleydenwurff.

Rebound and recovered in old boards, portions of clasps and corner clamps being affixed.

On 61 4^b, "Robertus Woode aldermānus Norwicj me possidet." In 1698 Cat.

H, C. *14508. Panz. II. 212, 221. Sinker. King's 31. Morg. 180–2. Proct. 2084.

OPPENHEIM.

JACOBUS KÖBEL.

6. 1512. JOANNES STOEFFLER: elucidatio fabricae ususque astrolabii.

F°. 280 mm. C. sig. S. ff. n. Title-page with architectural border and date 1513 against 1512 of colophon. Printer's device at end. Fine ornamental initials, and beautifully executed figures and diagrams.

Colln. Prelim.: *two* quires of *six* ff. (c. sig., c. ff. n.).; Text: A–D^6, E^8, F–K^6, L^4, MN^6=90 ff.

Rebacked with original boards and parts of clasps. Border on leather cover formed by roll stamp of winged dragon, wasp, dog, flowers and pineapple; enclosed panel lozenged by intersecting fillets (cf. Weale, nos. 77, 78 on pp. 112, 113). Bound with No. 70.

Verso of front guard leaf, "Simon Watson." Presented by T. Crosse in 1728. Panz. VII. 488, 17. Proct. (1501–1520) 11922.

ITALY.

VENEZIA.

JOHANN OF KÖLN AND JOHANN MANTHEN.

7. (1477 *Proct.*) ANTONIUS DE BUTRIO: super primo decretalium "a titulo *de translatione praelatorum* vsque ad titulum *de officio delegati* super quibus titulis dominus Abbas non scripsit, vel si scripsit reperire potest nemo."

(N.B.—Without date, printer, place.)

F°. 403 mm. C. sig. S. ff. n. 2 col. 58 li. Headings written not printed. Coloured initials.

Colln. Pt I. a^{10}, bCcd^8, e^{10}; Pt II. abc^8, d^6=(52+30)=82 ff. N.B. Pt I. e 9^b register for both parts and colophon, e 10 blank.

Bound up between Pt I. and Pt II. of No. 38.

H. *4172. Proct. 4326.

JOHANNES AND GREGORIUS DE GREGORIIS.

8. n.d. VALERIUS MAXIMUS: facta et dicta cum interpretatione Omniboni Leoniceni.

(N.B.—Without printer or date. Proctor places this after the 1483 books of the printers above-mentioned.)

F°. 312 mm. C. sig. S. ff. n.

Colln. Table: x^2; Text: ab^8, c^6, d–z^8, & ↄ^8, ℞^{6}=206 ff.

Bound with No. 23. In 1633 Cat.

H. *15785. Panz. IV. 205, 1246. Proct. 4504.

HEREDES OCTAUIANI SCOTI AC SOCII.

9. (i) 10 July⎫ 1518. GREGORIUS DE ARIMINO : in
(ii) 8 Oct.⎭
(i) primo, (ii) secundo sententiarum.

F°. 297 mm. C. sig. C. ff. n. Catchwords. 2 col. 65 li. Marg. At end printer's device (*Krist.* 286). *Type*, Goth. 20 li. = 72 mm. ; larger type for headlines.
Colln. (i) a–v⁸, xy⁶ = 172 ff. ; (ii) aa–oo⁸, pp¹⁰ = 122 ff.
Bound along with a supplementary vol. in smaller type, dated Venice 28 March 1522. In 1633 Cat.
Panz. VIII. 444, 893.

BAPTISTA DE TORTIS.

10. (i) 28 Sept. 1504.⎫ BARTOLUS DE SAXOFERRATO: super
(ii) 24 Nov. 1505.⎭
(i) prima, (ii) secunda infortiati cum apostillis.

(Bound in one vol.)

F°. 430 mm. C. sig. C. ff. n. 2 col. Marg. Interlin. index letters. At end of (i) and (ii) printer's device (*Krist.* 322). *Type*, Goth. 20 li. = 90 mm. ; smaller type (20 li. = 70–71 mm.) for margin, etc. ; larger for titles.
Colln. (i) a–z⁸, ꝛꝯ⁸, ꝛ⁶ (ꝛ 6 wanting) = (206 − 1) = 205 ff. ; (ii) aa–zz⁸, ꝣꝯꝯꝛ ꝛ⁸ = 208 ff.
Rebacked with old boards and portions of clasps. Two sets of three fillets forming frame. Between the sets is a tendril scroll with flowers of six petals and pistils. Enclosed panel divided by fillets diagonally, with fleurons in the partitions.
On a 2ᵃ, "Liber Ric. Layton." In 1633 Cat.

11. (i) 16 Feb. 1505.⎫ BARTOLUS DE SAXOFERRATO: super
(ii) 28 July 1506.⎭
(i) prima, (ii) secunda digesti veteris cum apostillis.

(Bound in one vol.[1])

F°. 425 mm., but in other respects uniform with No. 10.
Colln. (i) A–Z⁸, *A–E*⁸ = 224 ff. ; (ii) AA–TT⁸, UU¹⁰ (UU 10 wanting) = (162 − 1) = 161 ff.
On A 2ᵃ, "Liber Ric. Layton."

[1] Binding uniform with No. 10.

12. (i) 23 May 1506.⎱ BARTOLUS DE SAXOFERRATO: super
    (ii) 16 Apr. 1505.⎰
(i) prima, (ii) secunda codicis cum apostillis.

(Bound in one vol.[1])

F°. 432 mm., but in other respects uniform with No. 10.
Colln. (i) aaa–xxx⁸, yyy⁶, zzz⁴ = 178 ff. (N.B. Between ff. 5 and 6 is inserted a
leaf numbered 6 of 'Bartolus super prima digesti veteris' which does not belong
to No. 11.) (ii) aaaa–rrrr⁸ = 136 ff.
On aaa 1ᵃ, " Liber Ric. Layton."

13. (i) 10 June 1505.⎱ BARTOLUS DE SAXOFERRATO: super
    (ii) 18 Sept. 1505.⎰
(i) prima, (ii) secunda digesti novi cum additionibus.

(Bound in one vol.[1])

F°. 429 mm., but in other respects uniform with No. 10.
Colln. (i) AAA–YYY⁸, ZZZ⁴ = 180 ff.; (ii) AAAA–ZZZZ⁸, *AAAA–KKKK⁸,
LLLL⁶* = 270 ff.
On AAA 1ᵃ, " Liber Ric. Layton."

BERNARDINUS DE TRIDINO, OR BERNARDINUS STAGNINUS.

14. (*a*) 5 Feb. 1487, (*b*) 22 Feb. 1488. NICOLAUS PANOR-
MITANUS: super secundo libro decretalium (*a*) pars secunda, (*b*) pars
tertia.

F°. 411 mm. C. sig. S. ff. n. Catchwords. 2 col. 67 li. Coloured initials.
Type, Goth. 20 li. = 90 mm.; larger type for titles, but not for headings.
Colln. (*a*) Pars secunda: aa⁸ (aa 1 wanting), bb–oo⁸, pp¹⁰, qq⁷ = 128 ff.
(N.B. Some ff. of first quire damaged, but text unimpaired; qq7 is loose
and damaged.) (*b*) Pars tertia: aaa⁸ (aaa 1 wanting), bbb–ooo⁸, ppp⁶, qqq⁵ =
122 ff.
(*a*) and (*b*) in one vol. Rebacked, with original boards and stamped leather.
Frame formed by two sets of three fillets, with a roll stamp of tendrils between
them. Enclosed panel divided by sets of three fillets into lozenges, presenting
in alternate rows stamps nos. 7 and 8 in Plate II. In half lozenges at top and
bottom stamp no. 9 in Plate II.; at sides small circles with *fleur de lys* (cf.
Weale, English Rubbings, no. 63).
On aa 2ᵃ, " Ex dono mⁿⁱ Roberti Cansfield huius collegii socii 6° Junii 1596."
In 1633 Cat.
H. 12329 gives coloph. of Bks III., IV., V. belonging to this series, but does
not refer to this book. Panz. III. 243, 1003 applies only to *pars secunda* above.
Not in Proctor.

---

[1] Binding uniform with No. 10.

Georgius de Arriuabenis.

15. 28 June⎱ 1502. Responsa Mariani ac Bartholomei de
10 Nov.⎰ Socinis Senensium: Parts I. and II.

F°. 428 mm. C. sig. C. ff. n. (for text). Catchwords. 2 col. 71 li. Title-page. Printer's device (*Krist.* 183) at end of each Part. *Type,* Goth. 20 li.= 89 mm.; larger type for beginning of sections.

Colln. Part I. Prelim.: ABC⁸ (ff. 3 and 4 signed A2, A3; C8 blank); Text (Consilia 1–152): a–h⁸, i–l⁶, n–z⁸, ↄↄ2+ ⁸, A–D⁸, E⁶=264 ff.

Part II. Prelim.: ab⁸, c¹⁰; Text (Consilia 153–): aa–ss⁸, tt⁶, vv–zz⁸, ɀɀ¹⁰, ↄↄ2+ 4 ⁸, AA⁸, BB¹⁰ (aa 1 blank)=252 ff.

Bound in original boards and stamped leather cover. Frame formed by 3 fillets (middle one broader) and a roll of wasp, falcon and dog (?), with head to the right, flowers and pineapples. Another animal more like a dog, with head to the left, also occurs. Enclosed panel traversed by diagonal fillets enclosing fleurons.

On f. 2 (signed A), "Liber Ric. Layton." In 1633 Cat.

Panz. X. 34, 83c.

Bernardinus Rizus.

16. 19 July 1492. Santes de Ardoynis: liber de venenis.

F°. 423 mm. C. sig. C. ff. n. (exc. first four and last ff.). Coloured initials.

Colln. A–M⁸, N¹⁰=106 ff. (A 1 cut out close to stitching. Prelim. begins A ij. Text begins A 5.)

Bound with and after No. 17, in original boards with stamped leather and remains of clasps. Sets of three fillets form frame border, and divide panel into lozenges. In the panel and round the border are stamps as in Plate II. Nos. 2, 3, 4. In the half-lozenges at the sides of the panel are small circles enclosing a *fleur de lys.*

After colophon and register, "Thomas bonenfant dñs huius libri hic et Horatius successere loco cornucopiae." Not named in 1633 Cat., but probably with No. 17.

H, C. *1554. Panz. III. 321, 1532. Proct. 4963.

17. 25 Sep. 1492. Hali Abbas: liber artis medicinæ (regalis dispositio).

F°. 423 mm. C. sig. C. ff. n. Coloured initials. Last leaf recto, printer's device (*Krist.* 268).

Colln. Table: 4 ff. (s. sig.); Text: a–y⁸, z⁶, ɀ⁶=192 ff. (a 1 blank).

Bound with and before No. 16. In 1633 Cat.

H, C. *8350. Panz. III. 321, 1533. Proct. 4964.

Bonetus Locatellus.

18. 23 Feb. 1494. Boccaccio: genealogiae deorum; de montibus, etc.

F°. 302 mm. C. sig. C. ff. n. Woodcut initials. 13 tables of trees with woodcuts of deities. Last f. recto device of Octauianus Scotus similar to *Krist.* no. 281, but with black ground.

Colln. a–t⁸, u¹⁰ = 162 ff.

On front flyleaf, "ex dono philomusi Gu. Glascocke hujus coll. quondam Alumni." On f. 100 is an arrangement of letters which may stand for "Io. Randel." In 1698 Cat.

H, C. *3321. Panz. III. 349, 1762. Pell. 2468. Proct. 5052.

(For Heredes Octauiani Scoti.)

19. 28 Apr. 1506. Thomas Aquinas: liber secundus partis secundae.

F°. 309 mm. C. sig. C. ff. n. 2 col. 65-66 li. O. Scot's device at end. *Type*, Goth. 20 li. = 72 mm.; larger type for titles, etc. Ornamental initials.

Colln. One blank f., other half sheet torn out. Table: aa⁶; Text: a–z⁸, z⁸, ꝺ⁶ = (1 + 204) = 205 ff.

Old covers and remains of clasps. Leather stamped with border formed by roll resembling N. Spierinck's no. I. in Gray: Plate XXVII. A, but wider (27 mm.). Enclosed panel filled with three parallel rolls of Gray's no. v., clumsily inserted. The combination of these rolls affords presumption that the doubtful roll no. v. is Spierinck's (see Gray: p. 52). Outside border, stamp no. v. of Gray: Plate XXVII. B. In this book and others with the roll stamp referred to, the pomegranate has been deliberately defaced wherever it occurs.

On recto of aa 1 "Thomas Cantuarien," and lower down "Lumley." On guard leaf is a pencil note of the late Henry Bradshaw: "Abp. Cranmer's own writing. Lord Lumley bought most of his books, and gave many of them to the University Library." On the other hand, the handwriting in question is supposed not to be Cranmer's autograph. (See E. Burbidge: *Remains of the Library of Thomas Cranmer.*) There are several MS. notes in the work some of which are in a hand which resembles Cranmer's. In 1633 Cat.

Panz. XI. 515, 338 b.

20. 14 March 1505. Thomas Aquinas: Tertia pars summæ.

N.B.—This work, which is bound with No. 19, comprises
(i) Questions 1–90 of Aquinas, (ii) the Supplement.

In form, etc. it resembles No. 19, but differs in presenting a larger number of ornamental initials. In 1633 Cat.

Colln. a–z⁸, ꝣꝯ4⁸, ABC⁶=226 ff. (N.B. q4ᵇ, "Explicit illud qd. habetur de tertia ꝑte sūme..."; q5 Supplement begins; C quire, s. ff. n.; C5ᵇ printer's device; C6 blank.) Colophon, "Expliciunt additiones tertie partis sūme...Impresse Venetiis ductu Boneti Locatelli...Impēdio heredum... Octauiani Scoti...Anno...1505. pridie idus Martias."

Panz. VIII. 375, 296.

PAGANINUS DE PAGANINIS.

21. 18 April 1495. Biblia Latina cum postillis (Nic. de Lyra).

Printed and foliated as one work, but bound in 4 vols. Fº. 362, 360, 356, 358 mm. C. sig. C. ff. n. (foliation begins 1st f. of 3rd quire; f. 500 in error marked 400, and this error of 100 is carried to end). Catchwords used except in quires c–o. 2 col. for Bible text, with interlinear glosses and ref. letters, and comment. surrounding text. Woodcuts and diagrams. Five or six kinds of type on each page. Coloured initials.

Colln. Vol. I. (to Judith): a⁸, b⁶, c–z⁸, ꝣꝯ4⁸, aa–dd⁸, ee, ff⁶ (ff 6 is blank), gg–rr⁸, ss–vv⁶, xx–zz⁸, ꝣꝣꝯ4 4⁸, aaa–iii⁸=476 ff.

Vol. II. (Hester to Ecclesiasticus): kkk–ppp⁸, qqq, rrr⁶, sss–zzz⁸, ꝣꝣꝣꝯꝯ 4 4 4⁸, A–U⁸, XY⁶=304 ff.

Vol. III. (Isaiah to Machabes II.): Z⁸, AA–ZZ⁸, AAA–SSS⁸, TTT¹⁰=346 ff.

Vol. IV. (New Test.): UUU–ZZZ⁸, 1–43⁸, 44¹⁰=386 ff.

4 vols. rebound, vols. II.–IV. in old boards. In each vol., "ex dono reginaldi Bainbrig huius collegii magistri." In 1633 Cat., said to be in 5 vols.

H, C. *3174. (Cop. gives rr⁶, ss⁸ for rr⁸, ss⁶.) Pell. 2353. Proct. 5170.

PHILIPPUS PINCIUS.

22. 16 Sept. 1509. PRISCIANUS: volumen majus cum expositione Ioannis de Aingre etc.

Fº. 302 mm. C. sig. C. ff. n. Catchwords. Text and comment. side by side. Title-page with woodcut of Priscianus (?) dictating. *Type*, Rom. Text: 20 li.=109 mm.; Comment.: 20 li.=76 mm.: also Greek characters. Fine woodcut initials.

Colln. A–I⁸, k⁸, L–Z⁸, AA⁸, BBCC⁶, DD–II⁸, kk⁸, LL–NN⁸=284 ff.

N.B. kk2 wrongly signed kk3, NN8 blank.

Leather covered boards, stamped with Spierinck's roll no. v and stamp no. 2 in Gray: Plates XXVII A and B (roll 121×14 mm.). The pomegranates in the roll are defaced. In 1633 Cat.

Panz. VIII. 396, 477.

Vincentius Benalius.

23. 22 March 1493. Lactantius Firmianus: de divinis institutionibus; de ira dei et opificio hominis; etc.

F°. 311 mm. C. sig. S. ff. n. Marg.
Colln. Table: A⁸ (first f. blank; ff. 2, 3, 4 signed A, Aii, Aiii); Prelim. and Text: ab⁸, cd⁶, e⁸, f–m⁶, n⁸, op⁶, q⁸, r⁶, s⁸, t⁶, v⁵=139 ff.
Bound with No. 8. In 1698 Cat., but possibly already bound with No. 8 in 1633.
H, C. *9816. (Cop. gives s⁶ for s⁸.) Panz. III. 344, 1712. Proct. 5376.

Simon Beuilaqua, second press.

24. 10 June 1495. Blanchinus: tabularum canones.

Q°. 211 mm. C. sig. S. ff. n.
Colln. Prelim.: AB⁸, C¹⁰; Tabulae: a–z⁸, ↄꝯꝛ ⁸, A–N⁸, O⁶=344 ff.
On title-page "Williame Moone." In 1633 Cat.
H. *3233. Panz. III. 374, 1940. Pell. 2412. Sinker, 314. Proct. 5391.

Ioannes Tacuinus.

25. 1 Apr. 1517. Euclides: elementorum libri XIII cum expositione. (Also addition by Hypsicles, and Euclid's (?) Phaenomena, Optica, Data.)

F°. 310 mm. C. sig. S. ff. n. 42 li. to page. Title-page, first words in large floriated characters, and woodcut of the Good Shepherd in border. Geometrical figg. in margin. Printer's device (*Krist.* 326) at end. *Type*, Rom. 20 li.=107 mm., but Goth. headlines, definitions and propositions.
Colln. Prelim. with *corrigenda*: quire of 10 ff. of which 2nd, 3rd, 4th, 5th are signed 1, 2, 3, 4 respectively. Text: A–Z⁸, AA–EE⁸, FF⁶ (FF6 blank). In addition, there are 5 blank ff. at beginning and 12 at end.
Rebacked, with original boards and parts of clasps. Leather cover stamped with frame border formed by floral scroll; panel divided by diagonals, with fleurons in the partitions.
On first fly-leaf (unfortunately the name of the original owner appears to have been cut away):
  (i) "Et postea hunc emit henricus Redyng monachus Tamensis a balthazar bibliopola oxoniis. Precio etc...a° Salutis" 1528.
  (ii) "Et postea hunc emit Henricus Smith collegii regalis Academia Cantabrigiensi socius & Doctor Medicinæ."
  (iii) "Et postea Henricus dedit hunc Simoni Watson collegii Divi Iohannis Euangelistae in academia Cantabrigiensi alumno...1628."
Also on title-page "Sum Simonis Watson ex dono Henrici Smith an. Dom. 1628."
Presented in 1728 by T. Crosse.

SWITZERLAND.

BASEL.

Michael Wenssler, first press.

38. 1477. Nicolaus Panormitanus: super primum decretalium librum.

(N.B.—Printer not named.)

F°. 403 mm. S. sig. S. ff. n. 2 col. 60 li. Running headings in right-hand corner. Coloured initials. Woodcut on f. 1ᵃ.

Colln. Part I. 1⁸, 2¹², 3⁸, 4¹², 5⁸, 6¹², 7⁸, 8¹², 9⁸, 10¹⁺¹⁰, 11¹⁰, 12⁸, 13–16¹⁰, 17, 18⁸=173 ff. Part II. 1, 2, 3, 4¹⁰, 5⁸, 6–11¹⁰, 12–14⁸, 15¹⁺⁸=141 ff. A few leaves damaged, but text unimpaired.

Bound with No. 7, in old boards recovered.

On f. 1 "Ex dono mʳⁱ Roberti Cansfield huius collegii socii 6° Junii 1596." On f. 165ᵃ "Rolandus Brug (? Brun), prioʳ de Wenlock." In 1633 Cat.

H, C. *12309 (Cop. gives 316 ff. including first and last blank, but in the College copy the first leaf of the first quire is not blank). Proct. 7482.

Bernhardus Richel.

39. 10 Jan. 1482. Hugo de S. Caro: postilla super euangelia.

F°. 407 mm. C. sig. S. ff. n. 2 col. 62 li. (varies).

Colln. Matthew: a⁸⁺¹, b¹⁰, c–f⁸, g¹⁰, h⁶, i⁸, k¹⁰, lm⁸=101 ff. (N.B.—Colophon at the end of Matthew's Gospel.) Mark: a¹⁰, b–e⁸, f⁶=48 ff. Luke: a–c¹⁰, de⁸, f⁶, g–i⁸, k⁶, l⁸, m⁶, n⁸, o–q¹⁰, rs⁸, t¹⁰, u⁸, x⁶, y⁸, z⁶=188 ff. John: ab¹⁰, c⁸, d⁶, e⁸, f⁶, g¹⁰, h⁸, i–n⁶, op⁸, qr¹⁰, s⁸, t⁶, v⁷ (v⁸ wanting)=153 ff. (N B.—p 8ᵃ 2 col. 57 li.; p8ᵇ first col. 55 li., 2nd col. 38 li. with note "non deficit quicunque," text continuing unbroken on q1.) In 1698 Cat.

H. *8975. Panz. I. 154, 40. Proct. 7537.

JACOBUS DE PFORTZEN (JACOBUS WOLFF OF PFORZHEIM).

40. 1508. GABRIEL BIEL: in quattuor libros sententiarum (Ockam) in 2 vols.

F°. 277 mm. C. sig. S. ff. n. 2 col. 64 li. Marg. *Type*, Goth. 20 li.=67–68 mm., larger type for titles etc. Coloured initials. (N.B.—In last three quires of Bk IV., type 20 li.=69 mm., and different type for titles.)

Coll. Inventarium generale: Aa⁸, Bb⁶; Bk I.: Cc⁸, Dd–Ss⁶, Tt¹⁰; Bk II.: aa⁸, bb–pp⁶, qq⁸, rr¹⁰; Bk III.: A⁸, B–Q⁶, R⁸+Inventarium: quire of 10 ff. signed with Arabic numerals (tenth blank); Bk IV.: ab⁸, c–l⁶, m⁸, n–s⁶, t⁸, v–z⁶, AB⁶, C¹⁰ (b2 signed biii.)+Inventarium of two quires of 6 and 8 ff. (signed with Arab. num.). Vol. I.=232 ff. Vol. II.=298 ff.

First title-page, (i) "f. Robertus Wiart crucifer"; (ii) "Frater Franciscus Pouret bacale(?)oreus formatus prima licentia." In 1633 Cat.

Panz. VI. 184, 67.

JOHANN FROBEN.

41. March 1516; May 1516. Concordantiæ maiores cum declinabilium utriusq̨ instrumenti tum indeclinabilium dictionum.

F°. 308 mm. C. sig. S. ff. n. Catchwords. 3 col. 80 li. in Part I. and 79 li. in Part II. *Type*, Goth. 20 li.=60 mm., larger for titles, headlines, etc.; Rom. (20 li.=84 mm.) for introductory letters, etc. Ornamental initials.

Colln. Part I.: a⁸, b–z⁶, A–Z⁶, aa–hh⁶, ii¹², kk⁶, ll⁸=352 ff. Part II.: AA⁸, BB–PP⁶=92 ff.

Rebacked, in old boards and leather cover with N. Spierinck's stamps, *Gray*: Plate XXVII. A, rolls I. and II., but two rolls on end board differ in width from rolls in front. In 1698 Cat.

Panz. VI. 197, 161. No. 56 in Pellechet: *Cat. des incun. et des livres imprim. de MD à MDXX*, Paris, 1889.

JOANNES AMORBACHIUS, JOANNES PETRI DE LANGENDORF
AND JOANNES FROBEN.

42. 1511. ANTONINUS: tertia pars summæ.

F°. 307 mm. C. sig. S. ff. n. 2 col. 71 li. Marg. Title-page. Under title is a woodcut (*Heitz* 4) at foot of which are "D.S." Round the woodcut are architectural details, and from vine tendrils hangs a label with "Basilea (Basliea?)‖1511." *Type*, Goth. 20 ll.=65 mm.; large printed initials.

Colln. A⁶, B–X⁸, AA–QQ⁸, RR¹⁰=304 ff.

Bound uniformly with No. 65.

On title-page, "ex dono Leuini Benet armig...." Another name cancelled, probably that of Sam. Lynford; see Nos. 43 and 65. In 1698 Cat.

Panz. VI. 188, 97.

ADAM PETRI DE LANGENDORF (for Theodoricus Berlaer).

43. 21 Aug. 1515. PETRUS BERCHORIUS PICTAUIENSIS: morale reductorium super totam Bibliam.

F°. 306 mm. C. sig. C. ff. n. 2 col. 58 (varies). Marg. Title-page in red and black; ornamental border with "V. G." (*Urs Graf*) in corner, also printer's device (*Heitz* 62). *Type*, Goth. 20 li. = 78 mm., larger for titles and much larger for headlines.

Colln. Prelim.: AA, BB⁶; Text: a–z⁶, A–O⁶ (O⁶ wanting) = (234 − 1) = 233 ff.

Rebacked, with old boards and clasps. N. Spierinck's stamps; roll no. v. and stamp no. 3 in *Gray*: Plates XXVII. A and B. Pomegranates defaced.

On title-page, "Ex dono Leuini Benet Armigeri"; also "Samuel Lynford," cancelled but legible. On fly leaf, Will. Atkynson, vicar of Potton, Beds., is stated to have bequeathed the book (to whom not stated). It also seems to have belonged to people of the name of Claver, for the names "Arthurus Claver" and "Marmaduke Claver" occur. In 1698 Cat.

Panz. VI. 195, 153.

ANDREAS CRATANDER (spelt CARTANDER¹).

44. March 1520. IO. OECOLAMPADIUS: graecae literaturae dragmata.

8°. 150 mm. C. sig. Paged. Catchwords. Title-page, title within woodcut border. Printer's device (*Heitz* 94) on last page with date 1519. *Type*, Greek, and Rom. 20 li. = 85 mm.

Coll. A⁴, B–R⁸ = 132 ff. (N.B. "A" quire unsigned; H 1ᵃ is numbd 95 instead of 97, and this error runs through.)

This work is bound up with (i) a quire of 8 ff. (originally blank), the first wanting, (ii) the tract No. 34, and (iii) a quire of 8 ff. (originally blank) at the end of vol. Of (i) ff. 2, 3, 4 have MS. notes; ff. 5–8 are blank; of (iii) all except f. 7 have MS. notes. The flexible leather cover is much rubbed, but shows the stamps of N. Spierinck.

On title-page, "Thomas Wakefeld," and the owner has annotated every page of the grammar. In 1698 Cat.

Panz. VI. 222, 364.

¹ His name is spelt Cartander three times, and the device at the end bears the letters "And. Car."

FRANCE.

PARIS.

ULRICH GERING (THIRD PRESS WITH B. REMBOLT).

45. 30 Apr. 1500. NICOLAUS PEROTTUS: cornucopiae.

F°. 342 mm. C. sig. C. ff. n. Running titles, marg., fine printed initials.
Colln. Tables etc.: AA, BB⁸, CC¹² (AA, AA 8 wanting); Text: a–z⁸, A–G⁸
= (266 – 2) = 264 ff.
Presented in 1728 by Thomas Crosse, Master.
H. 12707. Panz. II. 332, 579. Proct. 8312.

THIELMANN KERVER

(for Jean Petit and John of Koblenz).

46, 47, 48. (i) 24 Apr. 1500, (ii) 1 Feb. 150⁰⁄₁, (iii) 15 March 150⁰⁄₁.
P. VIRGILIUS MARO: (i) Bucolica, Georgica with commentaries,
(ii) Aeneis with commentaries, MAPHEI VEGII liber, etc.,
(iii) Opuscula.

Uniformly printed and bound in one volume.

F°. 276–278 mm. C. sig. C. ff. n. Text and sur. comment. *Type*, Rom.:
Verse 10 li. = 62 mm.; Comment. 20 li. = 77 mm. Ornamental initials.
Colln. (i) Title, Table, etc.: a quire of 6 ff. (s. ff. n.) of which 2nd and 3rd
are signed 2 and 3; Text, etc.: a⁸, b–i⁶, k⁸, l–z⁶, A–G⁶ = 196 ff. N.B. Title-page
in red and black with plate of Jean Petit. No colophon, but Ascensius' introductory letter is dated from Paris "ad octauū Calendas Maias Anni. 1500."

(ii) Title, Table, etc.: a quire of 6 ff. (s. ff. n.) of which 1st and 2nd are not
signed, 3rd signed 4 iii and 4th 4; Text etc.: Aa–Zz⁶, AA–ZZ⁶, aaa–qqq⁶, rrr⁸,
sssttt⁶ = 398 ff. N.B. Foliation faulty; rrr 5 is signed rrr 4.

Title-page with device of bookseller Joannes Alexander (*Silv.* 66). Aeneid
ends rrr 8ᵃ with a colophon: "Impressum...ad kalendas Feb. anno ſm Parr-
hieñ supputationē. 1500. ſm Romanam vero. 1501." The 13th book of the
Aeneid by Mapheus Vegius etc. occupy quires sss, ttt; ttt 6ᵃ presents another
colophon: "...Quę omnia...coimpressit...Thielmānus Keruer confluentinus...ad

decimū calēdas Februarii: āno secūdū eiusdē loci supputationē M.D." Below Kerver's device.

(iii) AAA–MMM⁶=72 ff. N.B. Title-page in black and red with devicd of Jean Petit. Errors in signatures. MMM 6ᵃ Colophon. "...Impressa sūt haec oīa...ad Idus Martias post Iubileū." MMM 6ᵇ Kerver's device.

Rebacked in old boards with stamped leather and remains of clasps. Large lozenged panel enclosed in frame border, formed by a roll stamp of monkeys, dogs, lions, dragons, unicorns and fabulous birds. In design some of these bear a close resemblance to the unicorn, lion and leopard of Petit's and Kerver's devices. Round the frame and outside are small *fleur de lys* stamps. Fleurons in lozenges of panel. In 1698 Cat.

Panz. III. 335, *613; II. 333, 595; VII. 501, 15. Ren. III. 356– . Proct. under *Georg Wolf* (i) 8390, (ii) 8393, (iii) 8395.

(for Jean Petit and Johannes Cabiller).

49, 50, 51, 52. 12–31 July 1513. (i) Sextus liber decretalium ; (ii) Clementis papae constitutiones ; (iii) Extravagantes Johannis XXII.; (iv) Extravagantes communes.

Uniformly printed and bound in one volume.

Q°. 222 mm. C. sig. C. ff. n. Text and sur. comment. Marg. Comment. in 2 col. of 67 li. Title-pages ; rubrics ; headlines and some capitals in red. *Type*, Goth : Text 20 li.=64 mm. ; Comment. 20 li.=50–51 mm. Ornamental initials.

Colln. (i) Prelim. : 4 unsigned ff. (recto of f 1 Kerver's device, etc. ; on verso and in following pages is Johannes Andree's tract *Arbor consanguinitatis* ; verso of f 4 woodcut) ; Text : a–z⁸, ꝫꝑ⁴ ⁸, A–G⁸, H, I⁶ ; Tabula : aa¹⁰ (s. ff. n.) =(4+276+10)=290 ff.

(ii) Text : aa–nn⁸, oo⁶ ; Tabula : A⁶ (aa 1ᵃ printer's device, aa 1ᵇ woodcut as in (i) ; A6 blank)=(110+6)=116 ff.

(iii) Text : A–G⁸, H⁶ ; Table, etc. : quire of 4 ff. (s. sig., s. ff. n.)=(62+4) =66 ff. N.B. Printer's device on first leaf.

(iv) Text : A–G⁸, H⁴ ; Table : 3 ff. (s. sig., s. ff. n.)=(60+3)=63 ff. N.B. Printer's device on first leaf.

In 1633 Cat.

The above appear to be later editions of Panz. x. 6, 476 *a, b, c.*

IODOCUS BADIUS ASCENSIUS.

53. n.d., not after } PAULUS AEMILIUS VERONENSIS : de
21 Feb. 1517. } rebus gestis Francorum libri IIII.

N.B. Renouard places the book before 21 Feb. 1517, the date of Erasmus' letter to Badius referring to it. There is a copy of this work in the Bibliothèque Nationale with the entry "Emit Antonius Papilio anno 1517 cal Junii."

F°. 302 mm. C. sig. C. ff. n. Title-page with engraving representing "Prelum Ascensianum" in *first state* (see *Renouard*). *Type*, Rom. 20 li. = 106 mm.

Coll. a–s⁶, tu⁸, X² = 126 ff. (X 1 gives *errata*, X 2 blank).

In 1698 Cat.

Panz. VIII. 210, 2720. Burnet, I. 64. Ren. II. 2.

Wolfgang Hopyl.

54. 23 March 1505. Guillelmus Lyndewode: provinciale seu constitutiones Angliae (for William Bretton).

F°. 328 mm. C. sig. C. ff. n. Comment. round text. 2 col. 80 li. of comment. Marg. Interlin. index letters. *Type*, Goth.: Text 20 li. = 92 mm.; Comment.: 20 li. = 67 mm. Titles etc. in red, ornamental initials.

Colln. Prelim.: A–C⁶ (s. ff. n., B 2–5 wanting); Constitutions: a–h⁸ (c 3 torn out), i⁶, k⁸, l⁶, m⁸, n⁶, o⁸, p⁶, q⁸, r⁶, s⁸, t⁶, v⁸, x⁶, yz⁸, z¹⁰ = (198 – 4) = 194 ff. N.B. From o 8 to end an error in pagination. On A 1ᵃ armorial device (W. Bretton's?). On a 1ᵃ within a frame with foliage, birds, animals, etc. is an engraving representing the Trinity, etc.; on the sides are vignettes of Hieronymus, Thomas à Becket, Augustine, Ambrosius, Beda, and Gregorius; below are trade signs of H. Jacobi and I. Pelgrim. Outer border broken on both sides and in interspaces are W (left), B (right) in red. On z 10ᵇ printer's device similar to *Silv.* 1066.

(i) "Ricardus Cowall 1527." (ii) "Ex dono Roberti Sayer S. S. Theol. Bac. et Collegii Reginalis quondam socii." In 1698 Cat.

Panz. VII. 511, 99. Ren. III. 51. Sayle 6148. Duff, p. 196.

55. (1506) Constitutiones legitimae seu legatinae regionis Anglicanae cum interpretatione Johannis de Athon (John Acton).

N.B. Ascensius, in his prefatory letter, gives Wolfgang Hopyl and Johann of Koblenz as the publishers, and dates his letter "in Parrhisiorū academia ad idus Septembris anni huius...millesimi quingentesimi sexti."

Uniform with No. 54 and bound with it.

Colln. Prelim.: ✠⁶, ✠•✠⁶ (s. ff. n.; f 1ᵇ letter of Ascensius to Warham, Archbp of Canterbury); Text: A–I⁸, K³. The ff. of quires F *et sqq.* have been cut out and pasted in; F and I are complete, but there are only 4 ff. of G, and 3 ff. of H, bound in wrong order, viz. G 1, G 4, G 2, G 3 and H 7, H 8, H 6; all ff. after K 3 are wanting.

The same armorial bearings, devices, etc. as in No. 54, but the blocks of the border described have been interchanged, and the letters U (?), B, take the place of W, B.

On A 1ᵃ "Ricardus Cowall. Anº dñi 1527." In 1698 Cat.

Panz. VII. 518, 156. Ren. II. 52. Sayle 6149.

NICOLAUS DE PRATIS.

56. 5 June 1510: CICERO: epistolae familiares.

F°. 287 mm. C. sig. C. ff. n., except first two quires. Text and sur. comment. Marg. *Type*, Rom.: Text 20 li. = 102 mm., and Comment. 20 li. = 75 mm. *Colln.* Prelim.: aa⁸, bb⁶; Text: a–z⁸ &⁸ A–D⁸, EF⁶ = 250 ff.

aa 1ᵃ device of the de Marnefs (*Silv.* 151). F 6ᵃ Colophon :...Impraesse Parisius (*sic*) p̄ Nicolaū de pratis Parrisius (*sic*) morā trahentē In vico olearū: apud magnum ortum...."

In 1633 Cat.

BERTHOLDUS REMBOLT.

57. 1 Feb. 1515. Codex Iustiniani—with annotations.

F°. 395 mm. C. sig. C. ff. n. Text and sur. comment. 2 col. 84 li. in Comment. Marg. *Type*, Goth.: Text 20 li. = 89 mm.; Comment. 20 li. = 71 mm., and a still smaller type for index or reference letters. Headlines large red Gothic. Titles, etc. in red. Ornamental initials.

Colln. a–z⁸, A–Z⁸, AA–HH⁸, II, KK⁶, also Tables (s. ff. n.) aa⁸ bb⁶ = 458 ff. *Colophon.* Impressus Parisi⁹ Per magistrū Bertholdum Rembolt Argētinēsem Expensis ipsi⁹ socioruq̄ eius videlicet Tilmāni Keruer Librarii iurati Parisiensis et Francisci Birkmāni Librarii Coloniēsis anno 1515. kal' februarias.

In 1633 Cat.

HENRICUS STEPHANUS (HENRI ESTIENNE).

58. 5 Aug. 1506. ARISTOTLE: libri politicorum et libri economicorum, translated into Latin by Leonardus Aretinus and edited by Jacobus Faber; etc.

F°. 285 mm. C. sig. C. ff. n. Marg. *Type*, Rom.: Text 20 li. = 94 mm.; Comment. 20 li. = 73 mm. Title-page, device of H. Stephanus, list of contents, etc., and below, "Apud Parisios primaria superiorum operū editio typis abso-|| luta prodiit ex officina Henrici Stephani e regione Schole de||cretorum.... M.D. VI. || Nonis Avgvsti."

Colln. A⁶ (s. ff. n.), a–x⁸, y¹⁰ = (6 + 178) = 184 ff.

Title-f. verso, "Thomas Goddallus verus huius possessor teste M° Coopero. a°. 1.5.5.3 mēse Januarii." In 1633 Cat.

Panz. VII. 520, 174. Brunet I. 469.

59. 28 Sept. 1508. (1) JACOBUS FABER: in politica Aristotelis introductio. (2) XENOPHON: economicus (Latin).

F°. 284 mm. C. sig. C. ff. n. Marg. *Type*, Rom. 20 li. = 97.

Colln. ab⁸ = 16 ff. (b 8ᵃ colophon, || "Parisiis || quarto Calendas Octobris. M.D. VIII. || ex officina Henrici Stephani. || e regione Scholarum || decretorum."

Bound with No. 58.

Not in Brunet, an earlier edn than Panz. VIII. 33, 876.

LYON.

MARTIN HUSS.

60. 12 Kal. Apr. 1480. ODOFREDUS: lectura super codice Iustiniano. 2 vols.

F°. 395 mm. S. sig. C. ff. n. (each one of nine books separately foliated, but errors in Bk III.). 2 cols. 66–68 li. Running headings. *Type*, Goth. 20 li. = 73–74 mm., but larger type for introduction (in red), headings, titles, etc.

Colln. The quires in these vols. cannot all be determined, as they are very tightly bound, and the sheets frequently present no distinctive watermark. Vol. I.: Bks I.–IV. = ff. 339 (4 ff. blank); Vol. II.: Bks V.–IX. = ff. 340 (5 ff. blank). N.B. Bk III. f. 77 and Bk IX. f. 43 s. ff. n.

In 1633 Cat.

H. *11964. Panz. I. 532, 19. Not in Proctor.

PIERRE MARESCHAL AND BARNABÉ CHAUSSARD.

61. 9 Aug. 1514. BOETHIUS: (*a*) de consolatione philosophiæ, with commentaries (i) ascribed to Thomas Aquinas, (ii) by Ascensius; (*b*) de disciplina scholarium with commentary; also SULPICIUS: de moribus in mensa servandis, etc.

Q°. 251 mm. C. sig. S. ff. n. Comment. round text. Marg. Title-page in red and black with printer's device: see *Silv.* no. 1307. *Type*, Goth.: Text 20 li. = 96; Comment. 20 li. = 57 mm. Ornamental initials.

Colln. a–o⁸, p⁴, A–C⁸ = 140 ff.

Old boards and stamped leather. Frame formed by fillets and a roll of tendrils enclosing flowers of 4 petals and 4 pistils. Panel divided by diagonal sets of fillets into 4 triangles, each stamped with a half fleuron. In 1633 Cat.

Renouard, II. 210: "Boetius" no. 20.

JEAN DE VINGLE.

62. 23 Feb.⎫ 1500. P. OVIDII NASONIS heroidum epistolæ,
3 Apr.⎭ Sapphus atque in Ibin, cum explanatione.
(for Stephanus Guaynard).

Q°. 246 mm. C. sig. C. ff. n. (frequently in error). Text with sur. comment. Above title is woodcut of 3 panels representing "Ovidius" with "Antonius" and "Ubertinus" on either side. Printer's device at end. *Type*, Goth.: Text, 20 li. = 113–116 mm.; Comment. = 68 mm. Ornamental initials.

Colln. Prelim.: A⁶ (A ii signed A iii); Text: a–x⁸, y⁶ = 180 ff.

On title-page, "Harry Parker." On y 6ᵃ below device "ex dono domini Morleyi." On y 6ᵇ "Henricus Bruno," "Wilhelmus Byreth." Presented in 1728 by Thomas Crosse, Master.

H. 12214. Proct. 8654. Ren. III. 101.

Nicolaus de Benedictis.

63. (*a*) 24 Dec. 1500. (*b*) 17 Feb. 1500. Nicolaus (de Tudeschis) Panormitanus super (*a*) quarto (*b*) quinto decretalium. (*c*) Repertorium Abbatis.

Uniformly printed and bound in one vol.

F°. 412 mm. C. sig. C. ff. n. 2 col. 76 li. Running headings; marg.; but not in (*c*). Printer's device after colophon in (*a*). *Type*, Goth. 20 li.=81 mm., with larger type for titles, but not for headings.

Colln. (*a*) AAA–DDD⁸, EEE, FFF⁶ (AAA 1 torn, FFF 5, 6 cut out close to stitching)=(44 – 2)=42 ff.

(*b*) GGG–III¹⁰, KKK–PPP⁸, QQQ, RRR⁶, SSS–YYY⁸ (YYY 8 blank, UUU 4, 5 wanting)=(130 – 2)=128 ff.

(*c*) a–s⁸, t⁶, v² (v 2 cut out close to stitching)=(152 – 1)=151 ff.

N.B. Colophon after (*b*), "Ultima pars...abbatis Panor. super quarto et quinto decretaliū hic ‖ finit....Impressa p magistrum Nicolaū de Benedictis. M.CCCCC. die XVII ‖ februarii."

Old boards, stamped leather, and remains of clasps. Panel surrounded with vine and pineapple border (Plate II. no. 5). Lozenged partitions of panel show, some a thistle stamp, others a crowned two-headed eagle (Plate II. no. 6).

On f. 1ᵇ, "Joānes Laurans possessor huiˢ libri." At beginning of text, "ex dono mⁿ Roberti Cansfield huius collegii socii 6° Junii 1596." In 1633 Cat.

H. 12334. Panz. IV. 352, 251b and 251c. Not in Proctor; and (*c*) *Repertorium* not found in H. or Panz.

Jacques Sacon.

64. 17 Dec. 1516. Biblia cum concordantiis.

(Expensis Antonii Koberger Nurembergensis.)

F°. 335 mm. C. sig. C. ff. n. Catchwords. 2 col. 67 li., but "Interpretationes," 3 col.=68 li. Marg. ref. and letters indicating sections of chapters. Interlin. index letters in Gospels. Elaborately designed title-page. Many engravings. Printer's device (*Silv.* 548) at end of N.T. As in some of Koberger's bibles—see No. 4 in this catalogue—the cols. in the Gospels are much narrower, with wider margins for *concordances*.

Colln. Prelim.: aa⁸, bb⁶; Bible: a–z⁸, A–Q⁸, R⁶; Interpretationes, etc.: AA, BB⁸, CC⁹ (N.B. H 6–8 and AA, BB, CC quires not signed)=357 ff.

(i) Title-page, "Remember William Overton." (ii) On guard leaf, "Ex sumptibus Collegii." In 1698 Cat.

Panz. VII. 311, 293.

JOHANN CLEYN, alias SCHWAAB.

65. (1500.) ANTONINUS: totius summae (*a*) prima pars, (*b*) secunda pars. (In one volume.)

> N.B.—No dates are given in these works, but in colophon of Vol. V. of the series the date of printing is 1500 (*Pell.* 885).

(*a*) and (*b*). F°. 301 mm. C. sig. S. ff. n. Marg. 2 col. 69 li. *Type*, Goth. 20 li.=65–66 mm., smaller type for marg., larger for titles, etc.

Colln. (*a*) a–q⁸, r⁹, s–x⁸=169 ff. (a 3 signed with capital; c 2 signed c 3; f 1 and r 5 pasted in). (*b*) A–X⁸, AA–EE⁸, FF⁷=215 ff.

First title-page, "Ex dono Leuini Benet Armigeri," and below title, "Servire Deo regnare est." On a 2 of (*a*) and A 1 of (*b*), "Samuel Lynford." In 1698 Cat. Pell. 885. See C. Pt II. 517. Not in Proctor.

ROUEN.

GUILLAUME LE TALLEUR.

66. n.d. [NIC. STATHAM: Abridgement of cases] for R. Pynson.

> (N.B.—Last f. verso is printer's device, see *Silv.* no. 86. Le Talleur probably dead in 1492.)

F°. 315 mm. C. sig. S. ff. n. Marg.

Colln. List of subjects: 2 ff. s. sig. (N.B. At end of list "Per me R. pynson" in the larger type employed.); Abridgement: a–y⁸, z⁶, z⁶.

In 1715 Cat.

H. 15092. Cop. III. 288. Panz. I. 510, 30 (given under London: Panz. takes the device to be that of R. Pynson). Sayle 140. Morg. III. 625. Proct. 8768.

MARTIN MORIN.

67. 4 Dec. 1497. Missale Sarum.

F°. 333 mm. (over-cropped). C. sig. C. ff. n. Painted initials. Woodcuts.

Colln. A–E⁸, F⁶, G⁸, H⁶, I–L⁸, M⁶, N–S⁸, T–X⁶, a–c⁸, d⁶, e⁸, f⁶, g–q⁸ (q 8 wanting)=(280−1)=279 ff.

N.B. On A 1 woodcut border and picture of "Celebration of Mass," and illuminated initial with gold leaf. O 3ᵇ–O 6 vellum ff., s. ff. n. On O 3ᵇ and O 4ᵃ coloured woodcuts of Crucifixion, etc. and border as on A 1. On O 4ᵇ illuminated initial with gold leaf.

Bp Sherlock's bequest.

Cop. 4229. Proct. 8776.

BELGIUM.

LOUVAIN.

JOHANNES DE WESTFALIA.

68. 1480. JOANNES ANDREE: tractatus super arboribus consanguinitatis.

F°. 273 mm. (over-cropped). C. sig. S. ff. n. Woodcut trees of relationships with labels. *Type*, Goth. 20 li. = 116 mm. Coloured initials.

Colln. One quire of 10 ff., probably originally of 12 ff.

Bound with No. 3. In 1698 Cat., but probably with No. 3 in 1633 Cat.

Cop. 1033. (Hain's 1033, if description correct, is a different book.) Campbell 154. Holtrop. Not in Proctor.

AUSTRIA.

VIENNA.

JOANNES SINGRENIUS.

69. 1520. CAIUS JULIUS SOLINUS: Polyhistor (with annotations).

(for Lucas Alantse.)

F°. 290 mm. C. sig. Paged. Catchwords on last f. of quires. Comment. sur. text. Title-page with ornamental border and monogram L.A. Device of L. Alantse at end of text, and of printer at end of "Index"; on the border surrounding the latter are the letters HANS REBELL. *Type*, Rom.: Text 20 li. = 108 mm.; Comment. 20 li. = 72 mm.

Colln. Prelim.: quire of 8 ff. signed with numerals; Text and notes: a⁴, b–z⁶, A–E⁶, F⁴; Index: aa, bb⁶, cc⁴ (s. ff. n.) = 160 ff.

Bound with Pomponius Mela: de orbis situ (in 1698 Cat.), and Joachimi Vadiani Commentarii.

Panz. IX. 43, 235 gives a work of same printer and year, but calls it a Q°.

SPAIN.

SEVILLE.

Jacobus Cromberger.

70. 1514. Arnaldus de Villanova: parabolae curationis cum commento novo.

F°. 280 mm. C. sig. S. ff. n. Title-page with coroneted shield. *Type*, Goth.: Parabolae and dedic. letter 20 li.＝124 mm.; Comment. 20 li.＝81 mm.
  Colln. a–h⁸, i¹⁰＝74 ff.
  Bound with No. 6. End guard leaf "Johannis Cowellis" (smudged). Presented by T. Crosse.

ENGLAND.

LONDON.

William Caxton.

71. [After **2** July 1482.] Higden: Polychronicon with Caxton's continuation.

F°. 260 mm. C. sig. C. ff. n. (sometimes incorrectly). Para. marks and initials coloured red. Contemporary MS. marg. in red ink relating to chronology, sections, etc. from 11th quire onwards; besides many MS. marg. of different periods. Long commas are used in the 'Prohemye' and Table, on 34 1ª, 34 1ᵇ, 34 2ª, 34 7ᵇ, 34 8ª, 34 8ᵇ and continuously from quire 35.
  Colln. Prelim.: ab⁸, C⁴ (a1, a2 wanting, a5 torn off at nearly the middle) ＝(20−2)＝18 ff. Lib. I.–IV.: 1–28⁸, *28² (14 1, 15 7, 15 8 wanting)＝(226−3) ＝223 ff. N.B. 1 1, 1 5, *28 2 are blank; ff. of *28 s. sig., but *28 1 numbered CCXXV. Lib. V.–VI.: 29–48⁸, 49⁴＝164 ff. Lib. ult. 50⁸, 52–55⁸ (s. sig. 51, but text continuous, 55 8 wanting)＝(40−1)＝39 ff. Total ff. (450−6)＝444 ff.
  N.B. At end are 3 blank ff., the first being pasted to verso of 55 7, which is much torn.
  On 9 1ª "Thomas Wilson" (slightly cut); 22 7ª "Mary Wils"(*on* cut); 55 7ᵇ moral reflexions in verse written and signed by "Mary Wilson." On last guard leaf "Paulus de Castro" (ink faded), and under this "Mary Wilson hur booke"; also other writing in an unformed hand. In 1771 Cat.
  H, C. 8659. Panz. III. 554, 11. Blades 46. Sayle 19. Morg. III. 684-6. Seymour de Ricci: *A census of Caxtons* (1909)—no. 49. Proct. 9645.

RICHARD PYNSON.

72. 27 Jan. 1494. BOCCACCIO: the fall of princes (trans. by John Lydgate).

F°. 311 mm. C. sig. S. ff. n. *Eight* woodcuts at beginning of Bks II.– IX.; woodcut to Bk I. wanting. These were "obtained by Pynson from France, having been used by Jean Dupré in his edition of the book printed at Paris in 1483" (Morg. III. 225).

Colln. a⁸ (a 1, a 3, a 5, a 7 wanting), b–m⁸, n⁶, o–v⁶, A–F⁸, G⁶, H⁴ (H 4 wanting) = (216 – 5) = 211 ff. Two ff. MS. table of contents in late hand inserted at beginning.

On H 2ᵇ, "Doryty (?) Smythe." H 3ᵇ much scribbling : top a Greek motto followed by "H. Smith"; foot "William Holder etc." In 1715 Cat.

H, C. 3345. Panz. I. 507, 4. Sayle 106. Morg. III. 753. King's 195. Proct. 9783.

73. 12 July 1521. HENRY VIII.: libellus regius adversus Martinum Lutherum, etc.

Q°. 225 mm. C. sig. S. ff. n. Woodcut borders for titles, one (used twice) marked "H. H."; see note below. *Type*, Rom. 20 li. = 109 mm.

Colln. Title, etc., Oratio Joannis Clerk; Responsio rom. pont.; Bulla; Papal Indulgence : A–C⁴ (C 4 cut out) = (12 – 1) = 11 ff.

Assertio septem sacramentorum adversus M. L: a–v⁴ = 80 ff. (v 3, v 4 blank).

Epistola regia ad Saxoniae duces: ab⁴ (b 3 *errata*, b 4 blank, cut out) = 7 ff.

Bp Sherlock's bequest.

Panz. VII. 244, 65. Sayle 277.

[N.B. The titles of Henry's *Assertio* and *Epistola ad Saxoniae duces* are enclosed in woodcut borders, on one of the sides of which are the letters "H. H." There can be little doubt that these letters indicate that the woodcut was designed by the younger and more famous Hans Holbein. Pynson's border is obviously a copy—somewhat inferior in execution and differing in a few minor details—of the border, bearing these initials, which is employed by Froben in the edition of More's *Utopia* and *Epigrammata*, published in March 1518 (copy in the Grylls collection in Trin. Coll., Camb.). In that work there are *three* woodcut borders, which present features that bear a family likeness. The first of these, which like the "H. H." border deals with the story of the Tarquins, bears no distinctive artist's mark, but the second, of an architectural design, exhibits on the spandrils of an arch the legend "Hans Holb."

It is perhaps a matter of some importance to note that the same "H. H." border was again employed by Froben in 1519 for the title-page of a little treatise by Cuthbert Tunstall: *In laudem matrimonii oratio* (in connection with the betrothal of Mary, the daughter of Henry VIII., to the French king Francis) which had already been printed by Pynson himself in the previous year. The facts stated seem to bring Pynson and Froben into relation, and also afford a presumption that Holbein, who did not visit England till 1526-7, was favourably known to English Court circles several years previously.

It is curious that, though Froben employed the " H. H." border again for the title-page of an edition of More's *Epigrammata* which he issued in 1520, he had discarded it in the second issue of the *Utopia* and *Epigrammata* published together by him in November 1518. In its place, he employed a border which, in general character, appears to claim a different parentage and, as a matter of fact, bears upon it a monogram formed of the letters " V," " G " superimposed one upon the other. This is the cipher of Urs Graf, of which another example may be found in No. 43 of this catalogue. In the entry in the Brit. Mus. Catalogue relating to this edition (713 f. 1) is the note: " The title pages to the Utopia and the Epigrammata T. Mori are surrounded by borders from designs by Hans Holbein," but this statement appears to be in need of some modification in relation to the title-page to the *Epigrammata*.]

Wynkyn de Worde.

74. 28 Nov. 1525. RICHARD WHYTFORD: The Rule of St Augustyne both in latyn and englysshe with two exposicyons. And also ye same rule agayn onely in englysshe.

Q°. 183 mm. (over-cropped). C. sig. C. ff. n. (except last 3 quires). Marg. *Type*, Goth. 20 li.=93 mm. Title-page, woodcut with elaborate symbolism. Printer's device at end.

Colln. A–F^{4,8} (altern.), G–S^4, T^6 (T 6 wanting)=(90−1)=89 ff. T 5^b " Thus endeth this poore labour...with our symple notes and the profytable exposicyon of ye holy saynt Hugh de Sancto Victore by the wretche of Syon Rycharde Whytforde." After this a colophon.

Prelim. discourse and second English translation following: AB^4, C^6 (A 1, A 4 wanting; s. ff. n.)=(14−2)=12 ff. On C 6^a " The sayd wretche of Syon ‖ Rycharde Whytforde. ‖ Thus endeth Saynt Augustynes Rule ‖ alone. Imprynted at London in the ‖ Fletestrete at the sygne of the ‖ Sonne by Wynkyn ‖ de Worde."

On f. 15^b " Thomas Watson." In 1771 Cat.

Panz. VII. 247, 94.

75. 15 Feb. 1526. RYCHARD WHYTFORD: The Martyloge after the vse of the church of Salysbury.

Q°. 183 mm. (over-cropped). C. sig. C. ff. n. (ff. 98, 100 wrongly numbd 97, 99). Marg. *Type*, Goth. 20 li.=92–93 mm.; marg. occasionally smaller type.

Coll. a–z^4, ᴣ^4, ꝯ^4, aa–ii^4, kk^6=142. kk 5^b: " Praye for the wretche of syon your moost vn- ‖ worthy broder Rychard Whytford." kk 6^a Colophon: " Thus endeth the Martiloge with the Addicyons. ‖ Imprynted at London in Fletestrete at the sygne ‖ of the sonne by Wynkyn de Worde. The yere ‖ of our lorde god. M.CCCCC.XXVI. the ‖ XV. daye of February." kk 6^b, printer's device.

On f. 60^b " Thomas Watson"; f. 92^b " Philip Watson." In 1771 Cat.

INDEXES

AUTHORS AND WORKS

PRINTERS, PUBLISHERS, ETC.

ARTISTS, ENGRAVERS, BINDERS

INSCRIBED NAMES AND DONORS

N.B. *Names marked with † are donors*

Atkynson, Will., 43

†Bainbrig, Reginald, 21
Balthasar (bibliopola Oxoniis), 25
†Benet, Levinus, 42, 43, 65
Bonenfant, Thomas, 16, 17
Briggot, Thomas (?), 37
Brug (Brun?), Rolandus, 38
Bruno, Henricus, 62
Byreth, Will., 62

†Cansfield, Robt, 7, 14, 38, 63
Castro, Paulus de, 71
Claver, Arthur and Marmaduke, 43
Cowall, Ric., 54, 55
Cowell, Joh., 70
Cranmer, Thos (Archbp), 19, 20
†Crosse, Thos, 6, 25, 26, 45, 62, 70

Devey, Thos, 26

Fitzwilliam (?), 35

†Glascocke, Will., 18
Goddall, Thos, 58, 59

Heigham, Clem., 4
Holder, Will., 72

Laurans, Joannes, 63
Layton, Ric., 10, 11, 12, 13, 15
Lumley (*Baron*), 19, 20
Lynford, Sam., 42 (?), 43, 65

†Meres, Robt, 36

Mettham (?), Thos, 37
Moone, Will., 24
Morley (*Baron*). *See* Parker, Henry

Overton, Will., 64

Parker, Henry, 62
Pouret, Franciscus, 40

Randel, Io. (?), 18
Redyng, Hen., 25

†Sayer, Robt, 54, 55
†Sherlock, Thos, 1, 28, 29, 32, 33, 67, 73
Smith, H., 72
—— Henricus, 25
Smythe, Dorothy, 72
Society of Jesus, 27
Stevenson, Reg., 2
Steward, Robt, 37

Tangley, E. C. (?), 3, 68
Taylor, Geo., 26

Wakefeld, Thos, 34, 44
Warmyngton, Robt, 26
Watson, (i) Philip, (ii) Thomas, 74, 75
Watson, Simon, 6, 25
Wiart, Robertus, 40
Wilbraham, Ric., 2
Williams, John, 26
Wilson, (i) Thomas, (ii) Mary, 71
Woode, Robt, 5

ATKYNSON, WILLIAM.
    Became Vicar of Potton, Beds., in 1536 and vacated his living about 1539. The advowson of Potton was granted in 18 Rich. II. to the Abbess and Convent of Minoresses without Aldgate, London, and presumably Atkynson was the last appointment under the Abbess. (Information kindly supplied by Rev. A. Long, now Vicar of Potton.)

BAINBRIG, REGINALD.

B.A. 1506; M.A. 1509; B.D. 1526; Proctor 1517; Fellow S. Cath. 1516; Master S. Cath. 1526(?)–1547. (*Col. rec.*, *D.N.B.*, *Coop.*)

BALTHASAR.

"Bibliopola Oxoniis." Possibly the "Balthasar Churchyard, Douchman" of F. Madan: *The early Oxford Press*, p. 273.

BENET, LEVINUS.

Son of Thomas Benet (created baronet 1660, died 1667), of Babraham, Cambs. Levinus Benet erected a remarkable monument in the Parish Church of Babraham to his father and his uncle, Richard Benet, which describes them as "two Brothers, and Both of them Baronetts: They lived together, and were brought up together, at schoole, at the University, and at Inns of Court. They married two Sisters, the daughters, and Heires, of Levinus Munck Esqʳ." On a separate dedicatory marble, Levinus Benet describes himself as "utriusqȝ Hæres." (*See also* Burke, *Extinct and Dormant Baronetcies*, in which, however, there is no note of Richard Benet's baronetcy.)

Lev. Benet is possibly the "Mr Benet Junr." who was admitted to S. Cath. as a fellow-commoner in 1645 under Mr Lynford (*see* "Lynford" below) as tutor. (*Coll. rec.*) Nos. 43, 65, presented by Benet, once belonged to Lynford. Sir Levinus Benet, Bt, died 5 Dec. 1693.

BRUG (BRUN?), ROLANDUS.

The only "Roland" among the Priors of Wenlock in the list given in Dugdale is Roland Gosenall, who was Prior in 1522. A "William Brugge" was Prior about 1434–7, and " Brug" or "de Brug" are names which occur in early deeds. (*Monast. Anglic.* v. pp. 73–   )

CANSFIELD, ROBERT.

B.A. 1570–1 Trin., M.A. 1574 S. Cath. (*Venn*); Proctor 1588–9 (*Neale*). "Lancastriensis"; Fellow of S. Cath. in 1588 (*Coll. rec.*), and the inscriptions in Nos. 7, 14, 38, 63 show he was a Fellow in 1596.

CLAVER, ARTHUR, AND MARMADUKE.

See these names in *Alumn. Oxon.*

CROSSE, THOMAS.

Of Essex; admitted 1698–9; Fellow 25 March 1704; Master 1719–1736. B.A. 1702; M.A. 1706; S.T.P. Com. Reg. 1717. Proctor 1716; Vice-Chancellor Camb. Univ. 1720. Preb. of Norwich 1719–1736; Preb. of York 172¾–1736; Rector of Ashby and Oby cum Thirn, Norfolk. Died 27 Aug. 1736. (*Coll. rec.*, *Grad. Cant.*, *Le Neve.*)

In 1728 Crosse presented about 200 works to the Library.

DEVEY, THOMAS.

See *Alumn. Oxon.*

GLASCOCKE, WILL.

A Glascock of Cath. graduated 1574–5 (*Neale*), and the name appears in the Coll. register in 1630, 1632 (Wm Glascock of Essex), 1639, 1663, 1679.

HEIGHAM, CLEMENS (DE GIFFARDS).

The Heighams at one time held the manor of Barrow in Suffolk, which formerly belonged to the Giffards. This manor came into the possession of Sir Clement Heigham (d. 1570), chief Baron of the Exchequer and Speaker of the H. of Commons. His grandson—also Clement Heigham (suc. his father 1626; d. 1634)—must be the "Clemens Heigham de Giffards" of the inscription in No. 4. This Clement was succeeded by his grandson, also Clement Heigham (m. 1633, d. 1686). A son of the last, another Clement (d. 1714), was Rector of Barrow and was possibly the "Heigham" admitted to S. Cath. in 1658 and the "Clem. Heigham, Cath." who graduated A.B. in 1662. (*Coll. rec.*, *Grad. Cantab.* Gage, *History and Antiquities of Suffolk*, 1838.)

In this connexion it may be of interest to note that the Bacons, also a Suffolk family and associated with the Heighams, were represented in the College. The records show admissions of (1) Nich. Bacon 1634, (2) Nath. Bacon 1661, (3) Ric. Bacon 1669, (4) — Bacon 1670, Nos. (2), (3), (4) being fellow-commoners. These Bacons were probably the descendants of Nich. Bacon, the eldest son of the Lord Keeper and the first person to receive the dignity of a baronet. (*See* Gage's *Suffolk*.)

LAYTON, RICH.

1500?–1544. Educated at Cambridge; Master in Chancery, Dean of York, chief agent in the suppression of the monasteries, a reformer of studies in the University of Oxford, appointed to assist in the trial of Anne Boleyn and to examine into the validity of the King's marriage with Anne of Cleves (*D.N.B.*). Foster includes Layton among his *Alumni Oxonienses*.

The identification of the former owner of Nos. 10—13, 15 with the subject of this note is confirmed by a comparison of the writing and signatures in these books and in autograph letters of Rich. Layton preserved in the Cotton MSS. Cleop. E. IV. in the British Museum.

LUMLEY.

John Lumley (1534–1609), *Baron*. Fellow-Commoner at Queens' Coll. Camb., matric. 1549. Antiquary and collector of books. Gave books to Camb. Univ. Lib. and also to Bodleian. (*Coop.*, *D.N.B.*)

LYNFORD, SAM.

"Bedfordiensis." Fellow S. Cath. 30 Aug. 1634; one of the tutors in 1642–3 to 1646–7; ceased to be a fellow in 1648 (*Coll. rec.*); Proctor 1641 (*Le Neve*).

Lynford contributed congratulatory verses to (i) Ducis Eboracensis Fasciae: 1633; (ii) Carmen...ad cunas Principis Elizabethae: 1635; (iii) Συνῳδία...ad regem Carolum de quinta sua sobole: 1637. In (i) he is described as "Coll. D. Joan. Art. Mag."; in (ii) and (iii) as "Art. Mag. Aul. Cath. Socius."

The registers of St Benet's, Cambridge, show the following entries:

1650. "Thomas Linford the sonne of Mr Linford sometime fellow Katherine Hall buried the 18th day of June."

1650. "Thomas Linford son of Mr Samll. Linford Bap. Oct. 3."[1]

1651. "Mary Linford Daughter of Mr Samll. Linford March the 4th."[2]

1652. "Samuell Linforde sonne of Samll. Linford. Bapt. ffebry 17."

1653. "Samll Linford Buried in ye Chancell April ye 14."

1657. "Samuell Linford buried October 14."

MERES, ROBERT.

Matric. Sidney Coll. 1614; M.A. 1621; S.T.P. 1634; Fellow S. Cath. 1623. The inscription in No. 36 would imply that he had vacated his fellowship about 1634. (*Coll. rec., Venn.*)

MOONE, WILLIAM. Misnamed "Moor" in *Neale*.

"Leicestriensis"; Fellow S. Cath. 1597 (*Coll. rec.*); Proctor 1597 (*Le Neve*). Matric. Pembroke Coll. 1580; M.A. 1587 (*Venn*).

PARKER, HENRY.

Of Gonville Hall. Succeeded to Barony of Morley in 1556. Died 1577. (See *Coop*. I. 378 and *D.N.B.*)

REDYNG, HENRICUS.

Described in inscription as *monachus Tamensis*. A house was founded at Tame or Thame in Oxfordshire in 1138 and furnished with Cistercian monks from Waverley; surrendered 31 Henry VIII. (*Monast. Anglic.* v. pp. 403- .)

SAYER, ROBERT.

Of Suffolk. Admitted sizar, Queens' Coll. Camb. 1652; elected fellow 23 Aug. 1660 and retained his fellowship to 1671, holding in succession various lectureships and readerships. (From information kindly supplied by the President of Queens' Coll. Camb.)

SHERLOCK, THOMAS.

1678-1761. Admitted S. Cath. 11 June 1693-4; Fellow S. Cath. 12 Aug. 1698; Master S. Cath. 1714 to 1719, when he resigned. Vice-Chancellor Camb. Univ. 1714. Bishop of Bangor 1727, of Salisbury 1734, of London 1748. (*Coll. rec.* and *D.N.B.*)

He was a liberal benefactor to his College. In 1758-9 the "iron palisades" on the front of the College were set up at his expense. In 1755-6 he gave the sum of £600 for the alteration and refitting of the

---

[1] Probably the Thomas Linford (1650-1724) given in *D.N.B.*

[2] Among the christenings.

College Library, subsequently paying a further sum to cover the full payment of the cost of the work. Moreover, by his will, dated 23 June 1758, he bequeathed to the College his library and also landed property to serve as an endowment for the payment of a stipend to a library-keeper and for the purchase of new books. Two codicils modified the provisions of the benefaction to the Library in respect to the methods of its administration, but did not touch its substance. His books were removed from Fulham Palace to the College in 1760–61 (*Audit book*).

In the article on *Sherlock* in the *D.N.B.* it is said that "he left...his library, with 7000*l.* for binding, to the University of Cambridge." Nothing appears to be known in the University Library of any benefaction from Bp Sherlock, and the facts above presented show that the account in the *D.N.B.* of Sherlock's testamentary dispositions is incorrect.

SMITH, HENRY.

Adm. scholar King's Coll. Camb. 24 Aug. 1570; Fellow 1573; M.D. 1590; ceased to be a fellow about Mich. 1592. (Information kindly supplied by Mr F. L. Clark, Bursar's Office, King's Coll.)

WAKEFELD, THOMAS.

First Regius Professor of Hebrew at Cambridge (1540); died 1575, and buried at Chesterton near Cambridge. (*Coop.* I. 337 and *D.N.B.*)

WIART, ROBERT.

Described as *Crucifer* and probably of the order of *Cruciferi* or *Crucigeri*, known in England as the "Crutched" or "Crossed Friars," whose first cloister in England was at Colchester. (*Monast. Anglic.* VI. pp. 1585–; also see L. Owen: *The unmasking of...Monks, etc.*, 1628.)

WILBRAHAM, RIC.

No. 2 may have been presented by Mr Wilbraham, admitted fellow-commoner in 1679. Wilbrahams of Cheshire appear in the Register, two in 1639 and one in 1687.

WOODE, ROBERT.

Alderman in Norwich in 1577, and probably the same person as the knight and justice of the peace in 1580 who appears in the *Records of the City of Norwich* (W. Hudson and J. C. Tingey, vol. I. pp. 313, 318, 416). A Robert Woode was Mayor of Norwich in 1569 and 1578, and was knighted 22 Aug. 1578. (Blomefield's *History of Norfolk*; W. A. Shaw, *The Knights of England*, II. 79.)

A Robert Wood, who was admitted at Queens' Coll. in 1620 (B.A. 1623–4), graduated M.A. from St Cath. in 1627 (*Venn*).

PLATE I A

Koberger Bible, No. 4—*Front*

PLATE I B

Koberger Bible, No. 4—*End*

PLATE II

1. No. 3.

2 No. 16.   3. No. 16.   4. No. 16.

5. No. 63.

9. No. 14.

6. No. 63.   7. No. 14.   8. No. 14.

For EU product safety concerns, contact us at Calle de José Abascal, 56–1°,
28003 Madrid, Spain or eugpsr@cambridge.org.

www.ingramcontent.com/pod-product-compliance
Ingram Content Group UK Ltd.
Pitfield, Milton Keynes, MK11 3LW, UK
UKHW030905150625
459647UK00025B/2876